# Heart Songs and Distant Prayers

Also by Catharine Steinberg and published by Ginninderra Press
*Signs of Poetic Life*
*Poems From the Cradle of Dreams*

Catharine Steinberg

# Heart Songs and Distant Prayers

Dedication
For Mum and Dad

*Heart Songs and Distant Prayers*
ISBN 978 1 76109 180 3
Copyright © Catharine Steinberg 2021

First published 2021 by
**Ginninderra Press**
PO Box 3461 Port Adelaide 5015
www.ginninderrapress.com.au

# Contents

| | |
|---|---|
| Heart Songs | 7 |
| Distant Prayers | 8 |
| My Dearest Mother | 9 |
| Because she waits | 10 |
| Demise | 11 |
| Orphan Arms | 13 |
| The Philosophers Way | 14 |
| A Presence in Tsutanuma | 16 |
| Feeling blessed | 18 |
| Searching | 19 |
| Entropy | 20 |
| The Source | 22 |
| Sea Mist | 23 |
| Palm Beach | 24 |
| Santa Teresa's Brumbies | 25 |
| Daydream about Tess and Iona | 27 |
| Drought in Australia | 28 |
| Rain showers in drought | 29 |
| Evening Swim | 31 |
| Belief and Truth | 33 |
| Birthday Blessing | 34 |
| Alchemy | 35 |
| Listening to Nature | 36 |
| Black Ocean | 38 |
| Self-portrait | 40 |
| Waterfall | 41 |
| Savage Landscape | 42 |
| Shipwreck | 43 |
| Phantom Limbs | 44 |
| An Emotional Abortion | 45 |

| | |
|---|---|
| Religious Zeal | 46 |
| Going Away | 47 |
| Visiting J.S. | 49 |
| An Old Soldier | 50 |
| Parentless | 52 |
| A Thousand Curses | 54 |
| The Odd Pale Pinky Rose | 56 |
| Ephemera | 58 |
| Train Journey | 60 |
| Lament of a Wooden Plank | 62 |
| Unease | 65 |
| Cloudy Skies, No Rain | 66 |
| Fire Dance | 67 |
| Being on Death Row | 69 |
| Flood after Black Summer Fires | 71 |
| While You Sleep | 72 |
| Marvellous Creatures | 73 |
| Singing Above the Dream Tide | 75 |
| Covid 19 Time | 76 |
| The Love We Have | 77 |
| My Own Children | 79 |
| A New Spring | 80 |
| Blue Moon | 81 |
| A Goodbye Dream | 82 |
| Looking Back | 83 |
| Evening Birdsong | 84 |
| Sifting Seeds | 86 |
| | |
| Acknowledgements | 87 |

## Heart Songs

Leave us your whispers
And we shall nurture them
From the forest creatures
That spill from your dreams.

We will grow them like wildflowers
Up to the canopy of light
And the trees shall awake
To the shouts of your heart songs.

## Distant Prayers

Hope is a distant prayer
That we carry in our hearts
Like whispers and echoes
Hiding in the dark.

We sat together
And heard the words
We did not speak.

We are far apart
And hear the words
We do not speak.

Hope is a distant prayer
That we carry in our hearts
Like whispers and echoes
Hiding in the dark.

# My Dearest Mother

It's no longer a question of what to do
But to allow Time to take his toll.

My mother,
Now an ancient tiny elfin creature
Wrinkled skin round crumply bones
Won't last the next cruel Irish winter
In this house.

One wintery puff of ice cold wind, and
She will float away like quiet breath
A small rattle, scatter of autumnal leaves.

Nothing to clasp her to this earth
Except my sad old dad.

## Because she waits

Because she waits for us,

Perhaps we bring death?
What else can we do?

Because she waits for us.

She whispers at deaths door
A shadow in his waiting room.

Perhaps I bring death?
What else can I do?

Because she waits for me.

# Demise

The musty smell of death began
With a possum's quiet demise.
An odour lingered under floorboards
While rain fell from the skies.

Then there followed a friendships end
An illness in the chest.
Then a slow downhill trend
And finally your death.

Alone

Now you are sadly tucked away
Under dirt and mould and mildew
Dressed in your best party clothes
A good repose, burial and funeral.

While walking in the yard today
The smell of sodden earth
Reminds me of your death again
And little possum, lying in the dirt.

Alone

I am lonely for you too.
For a friendship that had grown.
Your love still feels alive and true
Like a scented rose.

Memories are the floral bouquets
Of our love and blossoming friendship
And though there's nothing left to say
We shall meet again some day.

# Orphan Arms

Your going is horrific.

Orphans arms stretch out
To touch you one more time
Forever yearning to be near you.
Just kiss me one last time.

Your emptied body lies quietly
Like a broken shell.
This is no celebration
But a kind of living hell.

You lie all by yourself
Abandoned.
In a strange field.
Underneath cold earth.

My poem is a comfort
Lying in the cradle of your arms.
A place now cold, where my life began
In the crucible of dreams.

Your going is horrific.

## The Philosophers Way

Kyoto

The Philosophers Way
Is walked steadfastly
With a heavy heart.

Noon sunlight slants through maples
Turning to autumn colours.
The stream flows by.

Beauty is remote.
Peace upended.
The oceanic gate is closed
To the deep.
The muse who gave birth
Lies underground.

*

She comes to mind
With the Dove,
Philosopher,
And Loved One.
Offering a doorway
To detachment.
Quietness descends in Ryoanji
Drowning all sound with clarity.

*

Noise jars, time distracts.
The garden fades
A veil is drawn over meaning.
Mourning is surreal
Buried under rocks, moss, gravel.

The heart is confused
So many paths.
Which one to follow?

\*

By the help of the dim moonlight
Go along the dark and quiet path in the field.*

---

\* These two lines were written anonymously on a small piece of paper that I bought from a fortune teller machine outside a Japanese shrine.

# A Presence in Tsutanuma

Aomori

You are here
Free to roam the forest
Like a sprite
Where light and shadows
Play with leaves
Blazing red,
Tawny orange
Pale yellow, icy green.
You dazzle
Dank dark furrows
And brighten undergrowth.

Buried treasures
Tinge blue in twilight.
Silver trunks stare stark,
Deep anchors to the real.
Spongy moss
Softly moistens
Pungent smells
Of leaf litter, sap, fungi.
Graves that give birth.

Water falls somewhere,
Trinkling, laughing.
In a daydream
The last white butterfly
Flitters by.
Small, with delicate thoughts
You ride its back
Waving goodbye to summer.
The birds have gone,
No funeral songs.
Flown south, like escapees.
You fly with them now
Towards bliss.

Your hand feels warm in mine.
Peaceful thoughts dance
In a patch of sunshine
And tranquility flowers
In a moon lit heart.
I hear your tread,
Your breath on my shoulder
Your presence very close.
Twigs snap.
I turn and smile.
No one is here…but me

# Feeling blessed

I feel blessed.

You've joined me up together.
I feel your presence now
In body,
In mind.
Like a door
That was forever ajar
But now an open prayer.

Your hands hold mine inside my own.
We are a comfort altogether
And we talk about the strangeness
Of the old, new.

A dam of dried-up tears
For years
Is full of life.
Refreshing water flows
Feeding growing places.

Old nightmares fled.
Long suffering ceased.
And for a while
Before you leave
You will inhabit a new world with me.
Togetherness one more time.

I feel blessed.

# Searching

I search for you in the mountains
Where wild eagles roam
By the quiet stream
Under shiny stones.

I search for you in cupboards
Under carpets on the floor
In between the cushions
Behind the laundry door.

I search for you in the garden
Behind the wooden shed
Underneath the flower pots
Old memories in my head.

I search for you and search for you
Throughout the night and day
And I think I understand it now
You have left me, and gone away.

# Entropy

I miss you.

Ah yes.

I feel the shift as I walk along
The shady path.

Cacophony of cicadas fade.
Leaves rustle gently
With a sighing hush.

Overhead wooly clouds coil and writhe
And hang peculiarly low
Like heavy pendulous breasts
A mythical maternal creature.

I miss you.

Ah yes.

I wish we had talked more.

Ah yes.

I miss our future conversations…

The quiet is blasted by a whining saw.
Cicadas crescendo
Cool breezes die away.

There is no storm today
Only liquid humidity before rain.

For an instant the path opened
To where you are
In a state of infinite simplicity.

But I find myself down here
Under heavy roiling clouds
In a state of finite entropy.

You no longer die.
I do.
A little every day.

I miss you… Ah yes.

## The Source

New words bubble up
Like fresh water
From an ancient spring.

Let's be together
Hold hands together
Splash together
You and me.

Waterfalls of poetry
Rush like winter melt
Down fertile rivers.

To the wild blue sea.

Let's be together
Hold hands together
Swim together
Just you and me.

# Sea Mist

Mona Vale Beach

The ocean whispers a million messages
Clapping and sighing from afar.
A sea mist circles all around us
As we walk along the shore.

The headland wears a milky shroud
Below a sky of powder blue.
A deep breath of ocean clouds
Washes away the moon.

For an instant we are wrapped in wool
And everything falls silent.
We walk and talk our many thoughts
But cannot forget the sirens.

That burden steals away our hopes away
The sand sinks beneath our feet.
But when we plunge into the singing foam
Our fears are buried deep.

## Palm Beach

New Year's Day 2019

Plunging into glassy ocean
Cleanses ills away.
The air, the clarity and salty ozone
Send nightmares all astray.

Through UV-protected glasses
The sea takes on a glow.
Restless movement on the surface
Reveals joy not far below.

My skin feels cool and tingle fresh
As I'm rolled around by waves.
A happy moment, deeply felt.
A memory to be saved.

## Santa Teresa's Brumbies

January 2019

Mournful ghosts sigh over a billabong
Where forty brumbies lie.
A ruthless sunrise finds
Relentless hissing heat
And loss of tribe.

Profound devastation.

Santa Teresa's Wild Wild Horses* died
Whole families fallen down
Crumpled softly all around

On cracked red dirt.

Brood mares, stallions,
Yearlings, foals.
No water left for tears. No grief.
Faded to silence in the night.
All gone.

A catastrophic drought.

Forty feral spirits depart parched land
And fly to ocean spray
Where white seahorses play.
Arching necks. Tossing manes.
Jumping galloping tides.

Forty wild brumbies dance
On lonely shingled shores
Wide eyed in the surf
Prancing in the foam
Twinkling into sparkling pools.

Passing into Dreamtime.

Heat hisses where desert devils
Spin their dusty spells
And rivers run no more
But who will grieve the passing
Of Santa Teresa's forty feral brumbies

In a catastrophic drought?

* Reference to the Rolling Stones song titled 'Wild Wild Horses' from their album *Sticky Fingers*

## Daydream about Tess and Iona

I find myself riding old Tess today
Plodding slowly round and round.
Hefty cart horse many hands high.
Wise eyed and chestnut brown.

Large hooves delicate on muddy ground
Her feathery fetlocks sturdy and sound.
For many years she pulled a plough
On English fields, over dales and downs.

I feel so small astride her back
And cling to her mane as we walk the track.
I recall her sweetness and gentle Iona.
Equine friends from a long way back.

I find myself alone once more
On a bushland trail in Sydney's heat
Balanced again on solid ground
I stride quietly along on my own two feet.

# Drought in Australia

I can't remember how to cry
Tears no longer fall.

Deep lush meadows
And watery skies
No longer heed my calls.

Shady places
In cool oases
Have forgotten me.

Flowing rivers
Now dried out dirt
Is all that I can see.

Whispering trees
In thirsty parks
Surrender hope like me

I can't remember how to cry
Tears no longer fall.

# Rain showers in drought

January 2019

Soft mist, light caresses
Fragile touch, spider gossamer
Essence of forgotten.

Dreams liquid into supple rounds
Moist skin, silken membranes
Fresh scent released
A faint memory.

Lacy shawls shake, spray
Minuscule droplets
Star showers bursting
Tender fingers like tiny dimples.
Indent and cry. Yearning.

'There, there.'
'Hush, hush.'

Quenched whispered promises.
Honeyed comforts
Of bees, petals unfolding.

Oceans far away, ripple in a single tear
Brimming over. Spilt.

And shout 'School's out'
As Sky River unwinds her silky sash
A wending blue sky wanderer,
Tumbling down in blessed relief.

Falling slowly
Spiralling like birds flocking
Murmuration and rainbow colours.

A sudden squall to kiss,
And clasp the hunkering land
That begs for water
Like beggars on a baking road.

Pattering feet dance dainty
On gulping leaves
Happy children chatter, splatter.
Laughter swamps pavements.
Roofs grown hard, dissolve

In dribbling rivulets
Gratitude is a joyful skip
A gurgle, smile.
Happy thoughts like moist milky mouths
Splash in muddy puddles.

'I'm so glad you came.
I can't believe you are here.'
I kiss your ancient hands
With parched lips
And the relief of one who has survived

The drought.

# Evening Swim

Water treacles cool on parched paper skin.
Slow motion swimming, extinguishes simmering fires.
A great whale breaches. Majestically.

A pair of shadow wings afloat. Expressions of regret.
Gossamer of dragonfly who lived out a silky life
In sunshine, and drowned.

Geranium petals crimson. Startlingly
Dancing, bobbing. Light as air on a mirror.
Ripples trickle away from finless, wingless fingers.

Humid summer showers and verdant grass
Steam under laden trees.
Flowers push against the weight of gravity.

To sky

Solitary shirt flaps helplessly. Tethered to a line.
Lonesome wisp. Old skin.
Forgotten image.

Faded voice

Ants blaze crazy over tiles, with juicy desert spoils.
Tiny messengers.
Motorbike riders, zooming on life's edge.

Evening drops her rustling curtain.
Big brown bird returns. Silent. Swooping low.
Her downy chicks cry. Squeaky.

Always hungry.

Baby monsters greet the end of swim.
Seed pods grin with leering teeth.

Reminders of your demise.
And that everyone is born, eats, dies.

# Belief and Truth

I would like to believe
In the song that grows
Out of tiny seeds by the lake.

I should believe
The way a swan,
Uncurls her neck
And trees birth many babies.

I could believe
If only I'd wept
For the wind that sweeps
And sighs her many sorrows.

But belief is hidden
Underground
Like the frightened rabbit
Caught up in a maelstrom of lies.

And while daphne showers
Her honeyed scent
Over bees that tumble
Near children that play in the sun,
A vixen cries her baby cry
As she creeps behind the moon.

Belief is poised to flower one day
Just like this song in bloom.
But truth gets lost along the way
As she creeps through tunnels of gloom.

# Birthday Blessing

3 February 2019

My Dear

What is lighter than gravity
And can free fall over a vast distance
Yet live?

An ant.

What can stay submerged in water for days
Inside it's own air bubble
And survive?

A spider.

What travels from one pole of the world
To the other, and then all the way back
Again and again?

Birds and fish and whales.

But what does it mean to feel immense pleasure and joy
When we all come together as a family
For one brief moment,
In the vastness of time and space and the universe,
To celebrate your birthday?

It means we are very blessed.

# Alchemy

When our different human natures meet
There are emotional storms
Like waves that toss crushed up bones
On unyielding rocky shores.

Deep suffering, bruises tender flesh
Along the cauldron's edge.
Thundering waterfalls toss to shred
Desires and wistful dreams.

The choice to live with this dark place
Embraces vicious pain.
To die means loss of treasured love
And the fight for a place in the sun.

The path to a peaceful, contented soul
May somehow still be found
Weaving molten stone and swirling foam
Into Nature's alchemy of poems.

# Listening to Nature

Listen to Nature.

The whispering wind.
Deep sighing sea.
A dove singing, at dawn.

Listen to Nature.
Open a door.

Shine a light.
Pull back the shadows.
Seek what you have lost.

Listen to Nature.
Open a door
To the universe.

And there you are.
In your own hands
Where you have always been.

Listening to Nature
Opens a door
To the universe.

The choice is yours
Set yourself free
Or, stay hidden.

Unformed. An illusion. A dream.

So!

Listen to Nature.
Open the door.

You are who you're looking for.

# Black Ocean

One day you cry.

The ocean is black.
Huge waves. Engulfing me.
The ocean roars. A terrible sound.

You cry.
I want to be brave. To enter the seething foam.

But you fall.
Dragged down by an immense force.
You. Small. Fragile. Drowning.

You lie on the shore.
Amid wreckage. Carnage. Beaten. Shattered. Spent.

You cry.
I feel like the littlest boy fallen from his horse.
I don't want to get back up. Back into the fight.

But how do I live in no-man's-land
A scavenger on shifting sands?
Grasping at crumbling truths above the alluring tide?

One day you say.

I shall dig for a spring and let the river flow.
Clear waters running into black
To see what lies below?

I say.
One day when the sea is calm
You will dive deep. To find the infinite.

And you say.
On that day I shall be strong. I shall ride the black horse.
I will dive deep. I will see clearly

And I shall find me.

I say.
On that day.
You will become the Ocean.

# Self-portrait

A whale drawn in black ink
Breeches the gold wave
Of childhood dreams.
Gold light pierces the mind.
Shining through a starry universe
A trillion billion light years away.

No one knows from where the light shines.
And nobody fathoms the abyss
From where the whale ascends.
They are here now,
Seeking you out
Bringing timeless images.

With your paints you want to know.
What lies below your star-encrusted waves?

The whale dives deep.

Swirling currents curl around a luminescent void.
Water shatters light from starburst showers.
Gold streams into turquoise turbulence.
Ultramarine surf. Cerulean storms.
Black fathomless depths.
White windswept crests far out at sea.

These are the intense colours of reality.
The ever restless, passionate ocean
Of who you are now. And who you dream to be.

# Waterfall

You were there again that day,
With your friends. In your mind's eye.

Where waterfalls cascade in sheets,
Down over the rocky steep.

You played close to the dark pool edge,
Laughing and larking about.

Then one of you slipped.

And in his stumbling fall,
He grasped for your outstretched hand.

His grip was tight. Nails dug deep.
In his frantic desire to live.

A pain keenly felt.
A kindness now lost, in time.

With a crash the image shatters.
Like silver spray over an endless chasm.

And I shall think about you in a quiet way
How we saved you. For today.

## Savage Landscape

There are ominous storm clouds gathering
Over the wild ruggedness of your face.

Shadows and light chase fitfully around
The craggy cliffs of your forehead.

A startled look of alarm whips up, like a bird
From the black lake of pain in your brain.

Smiles of entreaty follow flurries of frustration
That trample your feelings to mud.

Raindrops mist over deep emerald pools
Then splatter down outcropped cheeks.

Wind hisses and sighs down dark mountain valleys
And through whispering forests in your lungs.

Emotional avalanches spill over crevasses
And through frozen ravines in your mind.

The tempest begins to bawl and squall
And daylight darkens to ominous night.

Your cries are broken by lightening strikes
As you give way to the power of the storm.

Streams gather at last in the chasm of your nose
Just to add to the quagmire of grief.

And like a thunderous spring melt, wild words burst.
From the savage mouth of your river. Called Rage.

# Shipwreck

Washed up on a raging shore.
Nothing makes sense. Anymore.

A long voyage upended.

Wild eyes drowned in bitter salt tears.
Sun bleached hair clenched in despair.

Wrinkles. Scars of old sins.
Past wounds gouged in gnarled skin.

Restless shadows hide fossilised shame.
Memories of countless fights. All the same.

Knowledge has grown and you've been shown.
That for all the pain suffered
The tribulations. The prayers you have muttered.

It has been useless. Utterly useless.

And that is why you finally let go.
To sink to the ocean floor. Below.

But now you are carried by the incoming tide.
A helpless, hapless newborn child.

To reach this old port. In the storm.

## Phantom Limbs

Phantoms limbs
in the mind

are unicorns
fiefdoms
don't fit in
not my tribe.

lack of clarity.

feel who you are
look clearly

dive deeper.

a little eye
the wise one

always knew where I stood.

lack of footing
spinning…

# An Emotional Abortion

Slip sliding away…

I don't want you
To think…

I hope you don't think…

What were you saying?

I just had this thought.
That there is no one
To hold onto you.

Don't say that!
I don't want you
To even think about it!

Now where was I?

Slip sliding away…

---

\* The phrase 'Slip sliding away' is taken from a song written and performed by Paul Simon in 1977.

## Religious Zeal

I admire your love of the cosmos
Your curiosity about the universe
Your thoughts on bountiful Nature.

But then you take a personal God
And smear the fine grease of religion
Between the cracks in your beliefs

You should let the shadows protect you
From the unquestioning searing sun.
You should not seek perfection
In places where there is none.

# Going Away

And you,
What shall all of you do when I fly away?

So, 'you' shall gaze into the lake
That froze over
And frightened you greatly.

While 'you' shall fly away
Over the crevasse
To your new home.

And 'you' will keep smiling
Even though hate is still hiding
Somewhere in your heart.

And you, what shall you do?

'you' shall seek islands of refuge
On your journey
To a northern sun.

And 'you' shall yearn
To be loved in a warm way
By a kindly man.

While 'you' still hide your gifts
From spying
And prying eyes.

And me, what shall I do?

So, I shall gather you all up
And tuck you in, next to my beating heart.
Safe, beneath my wings.

## Visiting J.S.

Your head hangs low like a drooping snowdrop.
I want to sprinkle you with water
And bring you back to life.

Your eyelids rest slightly open, like pods
Revealing a youthful 'forget me not' blue
In your pale sapphire irises.

I want you to open your eyes wide now
Like petals greeting the morning sun
To smile at me. Refreshingly.

But you are in a deeper shade of sleep
Under spells of salvia and poppy seed
And bandages enfold your delicate head
Like widows tears.

I wonder whether you are still in there
Hiding somewhere?
Whether you are still here,
And if you can hear me?

I stand, looking at you like an anxious child
Clutching a bunch of violets
With a card of wishes, that fly to you like a bird.

I came to visit, but it seems you are out today.
Perhaps you are away?
Walking in the hills with old friends?
I leave you nodding sleepily amongst the flowers.

## An Old Soldier

For Dad

An old soldier collapses
Into gathering dust.

A strong heart lies broken
After relentless pain.

He groans the dying roars
Of a long lost warrior.

In a long gone war.

Swollen wounded limbs
Will not stand him up. Stalwart. Steady.

For one last fight.

He lies there quietly,
In the morning gloom.

'I am fallen.'
He whispers to an empty room.

His beloved gone before him.

Memories of happier days
Fading fast to grief. To sleep.

A withered colossus
Soon to be entombed.

But surrender is the signature required
To cross from this life.

And there is no peaceful dying
For this Brave Knight, of the old fight.

## Parentless

We are all alone. Parentless. Left behind.
Crying in your stone house.

Quietly in your last bed
You are laid out. Cold.
Silenced with no pin drop.
No one comes.

And you wait….

Alone…

So here you are, in this place
Where you last saw…
Her face
And how strangely she appeared
Not herself any more.

It was hard not to cry out.

In shock.

Your turn today.
Also with a strange face
Not like yourself at all
All tidied, neat, clean. Best suit. Hair combed.

Readied for the last journey.
A repose, before the flurry.
Of cars, flowers, mourners. The funeral.

You cannot cry out

In shock…

In disbelief, or relief?

We will pray over you. Your children
Cry and sing
Crack a joke
Remember you tenderly.

A rose fades by a distant evening window
And only when it falls, will she call for you
Only then shall you leave us behind.

Parentless.

# A Thousand Curses

Grey granite from Viking meadow built this gothic folly.
My folks lived more than fifty years, within this pile of stones.

Was it a grand love affair that knew no bounds?

Or…was it the bondage of a thousand curses?

Tonight's full moon hangs silver in the skylight
And all is deathly quiet in the house.
With only wandering ghosts as homeless creatures.

Big dreams have withered like the indoor plants.
Mould crouches in damp corners. Windows sag.
Cupboards swollen shut, with contents long forgotten.

Childish laughter just an echo down the hall.
A breeze behind torn curtains, a sigh wafting into dust
Scatterings up the stairs. A footstep in the basement.

He shouted at his old wife one day,
'I cannot leave my house! You mustn't sell! It will kill me!'

And so she didn't.

And so they stayed, and decayed.
All three. Together. She, he and the house.

Endless winters settled in.

Was it a grand love affair that knew no bounds?

Or…the bondage of a thousand curses?

Tonight the old folks no longer slumber in their beds.
Their souls have fled.

Tonight a listening silence roams the house.
A heavy presence wants to speak

About an endless longing.

To be free again as rubbled stones in Viking meadow

Far from the bondage of a thousand curses.

Or…was it a grand love affair that knew no bounds?

# The Odd Pale Pinky Rose

She was the toughest flower I ever knew
Bred for colour and beauty.

A hot house hybrid plant.

Her sisters all died long ago,
The bunch was thrown away.

But there she stayed, fresh all through May
Like a breezy summers day.

A rather odd pale pinky rose.

I placed her in a small green jug
Next to the window sill.

She turned her face towards the sun
And seemed to wait for you. To come.

A rather odd pale pinky rose.

Her petals drooped but did not fall.
I thought she would not last.

But even after you had passed
She held her vigil fast.

She lingered on for many days.
Why I cannot say.

Until one day, she took the jug.
And they quietly slipped away.

A rather odd pale pinky rose.

# Ephemera

What are you?

A glass bell without a ringer?

Deaf.

A glass lamp without a bulb?

Blind.

What are you?

Crimson hued.

Noticed years ago.

A passing glimpse
Then long forgotten.

Found today
Shrouded in dirt.

A buried treasure
Yielded

From stripping bare
The old house.

Her crumbling bones
Now a naked beauty.

An unexpected delight.

But what are you?

A whimsy?

Speak!

# Train Journey

Gordon to Wynyard

The new train exhales strangled groans
Like old Jurassic bones.

Squished together, we are sardines
Tightly packed in an oily tin.

Sliding towards the city in a line dance…

Passengers in a roomful of silent conversations
Swaying to our private beliefs.

Souls lost on mobile phones
Gazing into infinite voids. Silent oblivion.

Sudden laughter, explodes.

Hawk man observes the world. Hawkishly
From behind his book on hawks.

Soft cheeked youth stands. Shaggy and tall
In a Dr Seuss shirt and heavy boots.

Schoolboys dream beside the door.
They are not young soldiers going off to war.

Leggy schoolgirls stand. Graceful and sleek
Like gazelles about to spring and leap.

Office woman leans on steep stairs
Applying make-up to pretty cheeks

Narcissus of the railways…
While others flop in crumpled sleep.

There is a simple joy to be found
In the ordinariness of being.

Collaborators on a train journey one day
And how we congregate together.

Like minnows. Gathering in a stream.

# Lament of a Wooden Plank

Hello

I'm over here.
The wooden plank you see before you.
Part of a bench top in your local cafe.
Don't be frightened…

I'm the finest wood you can buy.
You can see my grain is very good quality.
That's what they said, when I was sold.
My annual rings are many and I'm very old.

But I still remember…

Fragrant air, cleansing rain. Songbirds singing in my boughs
All day in spring and summer.
Mist dancing round me, as the sun rises in my mountain valley
On frosty mornings my feet feel warm and snug. In deep dark earth.

I recall a swift flowing river where wallabies sip cool water,
And fish leap high in the air.
Possums play rough and tumble, wombats burrow in my hollows.
Insects and bees buzz around my flowers
Butterflies flitter in their thousands…

The ancient forest, where I lived was a place of sacred joy.
My family grew tall and strong all around me.
Life was good for many seasons.

One day.…

Men come with axes and saws.
They tear us apart.
Cutting cruelly into our limbs.
Screams and groans rent the air.
My children, brothers and sisters lie murdered.
All around me.

Then…

When the forest is destroyed,
They come to me, the tallest tree.
They look at me with greedy eyes.
I am terrified and want to run away.
Far away, like the forest animals.
But my strong roots hold fast…

Men tore my heart out that day…
My soul still lies there gouged and scarred
Hidden deep underground
In that desolate place
Weeping for me.

Mourning for all of us.

My body suffered terribly.
I was broken into many pieces.
Parts of me were scattered world wide.
I became furniture, paper, mulch.
And the plank that you see before you.

This morning I heard you ordering coffee
Eating cake, enjoying yourself with your family and friends.
Chatting, chuckling, whispering…

Like rattling leaves on an autumn breeze…

I long for that belonging.
To be a tree back in my home
With my family around me,
In our forest, with all our friends
But that has gone.

Vanished.

All I have left is this broken piece of me
And my dreams…

You know
At night when you have all gone home
I weep silently for my sacred place. For my dear ones.
Perhaps if I could see the stars
Through that window I might find hope?

But no.

I'm a broken fragmented skeleton
Nailed to a bench top in your local cafe.
Imprisoned in a concrete jungle
Where the air is bad and the sky is filled with smog.

## Unease

For N.S. 3/11/2019

The wind has gone from our sails.
Becalmed. In an exhausted way.

No tears shed
But a small leak threatens
To overflow. To sink us.

A thought grows. Unsaid.
From a hollowed space.

There's a man overboard.
A big voice gone silent.

Dreams lost in the wake.

But his many words are written.
Deep scratches in the hull.

Signs of a full life once lived.

Either way
There is an uneasy lull
With the wind gone from our sails.

With the man overboard
His big voice. Silent.

# Cloudy Skies, No Rain

December 2019

Cleaving the waters surface with a shudder
Knowledge hits home with a splash
That ripples of climate change begin quietly
Like the beat of a butterfly wing.

No rain falls from cloudy skies
Raindrops mingle with smoke dust
Cremated remains of Country.

Shadowing a blood red sun
Ash falls into blackened seas.
Milky Way, a memory.

Vast Gondwana. Ancient Land.
Mysterious Being. Violated.
Sacred places laid open.

Her children's screams fall silent.
Vanished into Dreamtime.
Nature's dried too deep to weep.
A funeral pyre to human greed.

A profusion of tears leave paltry, salty stains
On my parched and guilty skin.

# Fire Dance

Lying low in grass
You don't see my peeping orange eyes

Here I am!
Hiding at your feet where you tossed ash
Carelessly. As you settled back to sleep.

My eyes are hungry for you.
I smell your juices.

Hot fingers flickering, creeping
Touching here, little licks there.

Mmmm! Smoke. Hiss. Ssh! Quiet. Quiet.

A shimmy of delight
That turns into ecstasy
With a flare.

Oh! That – feels – so – good!

Pole dancing, up a tree trunk.
Crisping leaves.
Crackle. Pop. Spew.

Animals run.
Scamper. Scramble. Panic.
My hunger grows. Insatiable.

Bursting through the canopy
I'm cackling in delight.
Can you hear me sing?

I'm huge. Beautiful
The forest explodes
With a roar!

You awake in fright
And try to take flight.

Too late! I'm here!

# Being on Death Row

bushfires, 2020

The pellucidity of thick green leaves
At twilight

Imprints thirsty eyes with clarity.

Saturation of colours impress
As an infrared sun

Sinks

Behind rising smoke from the south.

Intensity lives a moment

In the quiet heavy
Of a humid evening.

Each intake of breath.

Sacred.

Sounds of precious water trickle
Through ears like a lullaby.

Below a row of citrus
Beetles scurry from a sudden flood.

In tall cedars black parrots cry like babies
Or are they wedge-tailed eagles?

Crickets buzz harmoniously
A background requiem choir.

Light puffs, cool breezes
Caress skin like goodnight kisses.

Senses spring greedily to lap up life.

Acute with the knowledge,
Of being on death row.

That such beauty in the natural world.

Will soon be lost.

# Flood after Black Summer Fires

2020

Here on the mountain there is bore water
That bores holes in copper pipes.

Here on the Ridge there's a difference
In the way wild things grow feral after flood.

Mind you, Nature's in charge.

Here on the farm a diamond python sheds his skin,
And possum hides his smell in a shed
And drains block when it pelts with rain.

Here on the mountain
In flooded fields, frogs sing in the Eden Garden Choir
And frill neck lizards swim in bursting dams.

And it is here on the Ridge
That in our conversations we wonder

Where the rain comes from so severely
After years of drought.

And here on the farm is it too late
For life to spring back after Black Summer fires?

Mind you, by the look of it, Nature's still in charge.

## While You Sleep

A blade of grass spreads
Like a crow's foot.
The lyre bird hoots at dawn.

Buds spill into blossom showers
That flirt with honey suckers
Humming with dreams of nectar.

Down by the weedy furrows
Mice have a field day
While the python is away.

Nature continues on its path
In the quiet moist meadows
Under the crescent moon.

It all goes on without you.
Above, below and around you
While you slumber.

Not where you think
It should be happening
Before your wakeful eyes.

# Marvellous Creatures

February 2020

Oh! Marvellous creatures!

After the drought. Drought. And more drought.

After the fire. Fire. And more fire.

After the rain. Rain. And more rain.

You have made it through Hell's gates
Through drought and fire, and issued from the flood.

Frogs! Throbbing with a thousand songs.
Throb. Throbbing. And more throbbing.

And one small voice shouting. Off-key. Slightly out of step.
How have you survived in silence, all these years?

Flying foxes! Flap, flapping leathery wings in date trees
Clicking your indignation as you eat. Greedily.

How have you survived the odds
Busy with the industry of living?

I am bitten out of reverie
By a thousand hungry mouths. Invisible insects
With tiny. Sharp. Teeth.

How have you survived to drink my blood?

And kookaburra! Laughing. Laughing. And more laughing.
Laugh your dark humour
And close up this humid twilight.

Nature's noisy little marvels. All voice. And hungry mouths.

Not one goes quietly, tonight.

# Singing Above the Dream Tide

Drifting aimlessly on shifting sands
brings to mind
A longing for rebirth.

The return to purity.

To pierce
the encumbered swollen sac
of overarching shadows.

To fly above memories,
entangled mercilessly
in paralytic guilt.

And sail through backwaters
of fear and shame
that still exist.

For

No

Good

Reason.

To peel back membranes
of the long dark night
and reveal a pale new dawn.

To wake and find,
a sunny carefree child
singing above the dream tide.

# Covid 19 Time

Nature awakens in the silence
Of self-isolation.
Clouds cumulate gloriously.
No planes, trains or automobiles.

It's Covid time
Self-distancing out walking
And it's Good Friday.

What should we do?
Worship nature again?
Take time. To dream. Let go.

Hissing grows in ears lost in solitude
Like distant traffic behind the quiet
Reminders of climate change.

Can we wind back the desolation
Of drought, fire and floods?
To find another Passover story
Far cry from a resurrection.

Who will lead us now
To the promised land?

And which of us will be sacrificed
As the Pascal lambs of tomorrow?

## The Love We Have

My love,
The love we have, is a lifetime of joy and laughter,
Angry fears, sad tears.

Together we abide as the sun rises and sets. Rises and sets.
As the moon waxes and wanes. Waxes and wanes.

And the stars churn dizzily in a dance
In time with the thrumming beat of the turning earth.

Brightly careering like swallows above our heads
Returning each day to their nests in the west.

My love,
The love we have, grows as our hair greys together
And mingles like ash and snow. Ash and snow.

With the seasonal harvest of reap and sow. Reap and sow.

And bones once young, crumble like sandstone into sand,
After the babies and youths. Babies and youths

Have come and gone. Come and gone.

Decades shall pass and fall. Pass and fall
From our grasp like gossamer.

And the ocean's tides retreat and return. Retreat and return

My love,
We will get lost together in the silent dust

Forgotten minuscule members of earth
Engulfed by desert or the rain forest story.

But the love we have, will be written forever as scratches
In rocks and stones. Rocks and stones.

And in the country of ochre as music,
And in fossil poetry as our songs.

A Dreamtime of resonant atoms lie buried
To be found much later in the fertile thoughts left behind

That we wrote intimately together as we lay in our many embraces
And wove the seeds and flowers. Seeds and flowers
Into the love we shall always have. My love.

# My Own Children

You may never know the explosion of love I felt
When I beheld you in my arms at your beginnings.
My cherubs.

When I gazed at you in your opened membranes,
Your discarded wings, after such a long journey.
My doves.

And as you travelled through an infinite universe
To reach a home in me. Always so near and yet so far.
My darlings.

But you were always here inside, silently growing,
So tender, complete and round.
My dearest dears.

I have sheltered you all along and yet you each remained
An enigma until your births.
My babies.

What sweet strangers you are that bring me these experiences,
Beyond my present knowing.
My children.

You are, in your perfections, as you have always been.
Peacefully waiting for me to wake from my slumbers.
My sweetest hearts.

Love and death and everything in between
Is all that I have lived with you and more
My most treasured souls.

# A New Spring

A feeling of flying
Lightly.
Youth leaps into step
With limber limbs.

Garblings of the ancients
Collapse
Into an old-boned pile
And the spew of dust.

The sun beats hard,
Mercilessly
Above the under cool
Of pale new leaves.

On baking boulevards
Humanity scoffs
At its own extinction.

Pigeons gaze
At our strident struttings.
Sharp eyes, knowing.

And I think about you
Whole. Entire.
In the bloom of womanhood.

Your long life running ahead
Facing the rising sap
Of a new spring.

## Blue Moon

I think of You, both halves of You.
Your long lives lived.

And I think of You, both halves of You
That gave me life. Watched me grow.
Then let me go.

A shadowed orb.

Yearning to come home to You.
But no one there. No one, no more.
No place to find You anywhere.

A shadowed orb.

Trees ripple in the gusty wind
Then orange, in the twilight sun.
Blue moon ascends into the sky

A shadowed orb.

In April gone two years ago
I farewelled one half of you
But did not return.
To comfort sad and lonely you.

Oh! How I miss both halves of You.
No heart can hold so many tears.
Our souls are now forever parted.
By endless tides. A thousand seas.

Blue moon gaze on their grave. Again.
And kiss them at your journey's end.

# A Goodbye Dream

I see you both
Ahead
On the other side of light.

Stay with me! Don't leave me by my lonesome.

You return with outstretched arms
Love in your eyes.
For me. Your tiny child.
'You will follow later,' you say. And kiss me smilingly.

No! Stay with me! Don't leave me by my lonesome.

I see you both
Ahead
On the other side of light.

Crabs throng on a vast beach. Clicking and clacking
Flickering and shimmering
An unreachable distance spreads out between us.

Stay with me! Don't leave me by my lonesome.

Looking back at me. You wave goodbye
To me. Your tiny child.
'You will follow later. Much later,' you say smilingly.

Walking hand in hand. Enfolded in your love.
You both walk on ahead. To the other side of light.

No! Don't go! Stay with me!
Don't leave me by my lonesome.

# Looking Back

Looking back

I still hear your quiet voice
And although your words are now lost to me,
The memory of them is a comfort to my heart.

When I thought I was running mad
You listened to me,
Endlessly.

When I thought I was slowly dying
You saved me,
Every day.

When I thought I was completely lost
You found me and never gave up hope.

When I thought I was frozen
You brought me back to life and love.

And although I can no longer clearly see your face.
I remember the kindness in your eyes.

We never touched
But I remember the warmth of your emotional embraces.

And while I believe that you know me very well,
You remain both familiar and enigmatic to me.

# Evening Birdsong

It is evening
The birds are singing
Can you hear them?

Yes, the evening is coming.
No, I cannot hear the birdsong.

The moment of a sad farewell
Is laid down in memory.
Only a hollow silence
Follows in its wake.

Where once there was life
There is a vacant space.
Now that we have gone.

Yes the evening is coming.
No, I cannot hear the birdsong.

Where once the day seemed long
And time was warm and generous,
There is an empty nothing.

The goodbye moment
And a thousand others
Cannot be snatched back.
Receding at the speed of light.

Yes, evening is coming
No, I cannot hear the birdsong.

I do remember how crickets
Used to tune their hopeful violins
But, they shall sleep till summer
Should it ever come again.

Yes, it is evening.
No, I cannot hear the birdsong.
Sadness is deafening
Now that we have gone.

# Sifting Seeds

I shelter in the arms
Of poetry
Against the howling storms.

I find comfort on a tranquil day
Between your words
And the blossomed boughs.

Thoughts spring up
Like distant prayers
When I seek you after your going.

No more to reach you
Or what's familiar
Has passed grasping, touching.

I find a lonely comfort
In the poesy
That come in a long line from you.

There is a harbour
To be found between the sheaths of words
Where I sit with you.

Sifting seeds.

# Acknowledgements

Thank you to Stephen and Brenda at Ginninderra Press for continuing to publish my poetry. This has been very heartening. Each book has become a map that locates important crossroads in my life and across time.

*Heart Songs and Distant Prayers* is dedicated to my parents, Francis and Patricia, who have both passed away within the last couple of years. This book acknowledges the sadness I continue to feel on losing them. The act of writing poems about my parents, my family and all that they mean to me is personal, but it is also an act of either celebration or consolation for what is found in life and what is lost.

*Heart Songs and Distant Prayers* also tries to capture the suffering and resilience experienced by Australia, its plants, animals and humans after the 2019/2020 megafires and floods. Most of the country is still in drought and we are still recovering from losing everything in the fires including loved ones. Worsening droughts, fires and floods will indelibly shape our external and internal landscapes.

Finally, *Heart Songs and Distant Prayers* is a plea for humanity in these times of pandemics, climate change, mass extinctions, social unrest and global economic crises.

Out here in the middle of a vast nowhere, this tiny blue dot continues to sustain life against the odds. All we have is each other, and what this beautiful planet continues to provide.

www.ingramcontent.com/pod-product-compliance
Lightning Source LLC
Chambersburg PA
CBHW062142100526
44589CB00014B/1670